Transparent Faith

Lessons Learned from the Plan of Faith

◆TRANSPARENT◆

FAITH

Sherrell Moore-Tucker

GOOD SUCCESS PUBLISHING

Transparent Faith
©2016 by Sherrell Moore-Tucker.

This book is also available as an ebook.

Visit www.sherrellmooretucker.com

Requests for information should be addressed to:

Good Success Publishing,
P.O. Box 5072, Upper Marlboro, MD 20775

ISBN 978-0-9837895-8-1

Library of Congress Control Number: 2016934878

This book is printed on acid-free paper

Cover design: August Pride, LLC
Interior design: Electronic Quill Publishing Services
Printed in the United States of America

Special Dedication

To the Liturgical Dance Ministry at the First Baptist Church of Glenarden, thank you for welcoming me into your family.

Dedication

To my mother, Rosie Moore, who raised me in the church and taught me about God at an early age. You set the foundation for life and never let me forget the source of my help no matter how far I strayed. You are my angel here on earth.

To my father, Arthur Moore III, you cultivated my love for music. Your ability to play by ear amazes me and I am forever grateful for my childhood memories of music and melodies in the house.

To my brother Arthur Moore IV, you inspired me when you left the military and followed your dreams to L.A. I was captivated by your courage but secretly fearful of your moving so far away. As my little brother, you don't know it but you gave me the courage to dream again. Your fearlessness is a testament to the faith that mom instilled in us both. You have already accomplished so much and I know there is so much more in store for you.

To my husband, Leon Tucker, you are my calm, my laughter, and my friend. You accept me, flaws and all. Your wisdom and humility provide our family with a solid foundation that I am so grateful for each and every day. Your love is a gift that I gladly open each morning.

To the U.S. Army, thank you for teaching me selfless service to God and my country. Also, God bless the service members who sacrifice to serve our great country daily.

Table of Contents

Foreword

The journey of coming to know God for yourself is just that, a journey. Like Sherrell Moore-Tucker, I too came to know Christ as my Lord and Savior at a young age. And like Sherrell I had backslidden soon after leaving High School. In fact, I learned rather quickly that the strong religious upbringing of my youth was no match for the pressures that faced me in early adulthood. Why? Because I had not yet learned how to be in a relationship with Jesus.

In the pages of this book, Sherrell encourages the backslidden and guides most everyone else through the process of moving from religion to relationship. In a way that only Sherrell can, she uses her power of persuasion and her years as a wellness advocate and coach to inspire the everyday believer to be more, do more and live his/her best life.

The race is not given to the swift or to the strong, but to he that endures to the end. Rest assured that no matter how far you've drifted from the Lord, there is a way back. Let "Transparent Faith" lead the way.

Dr. Celeste C. Owens
Speaker and Author of "*The 40-Day Surrender Fast*"

Introduction

In April 2009, I repented, joined the First Baptist Church of Glenarden, and got baptized. That decision changed the course of my life forever.

Through the teachings of Pastor John K. Jenkins, Sr., Bishop T.D. Jakes, Pastor Keith Battle, Bible Institute classes, focus study classes, my family, my church family, and countless others I began to understand my new life in Christ, God's plan for my life, and the process that God uses to birth purpose.

In the next few chapters of this book, I will share some stories of transparency in hopes that the lessons will help new Christians understand God's divine plan and process for living a life of purpose.

My Story:
Confessions of a Backslider

All of us also lived among them at one time, gratifying the
cravings of our flesh and following its desires and thoughts.
Like the rest, we were by nature deserving of wrath. But
because of His great love for us, God, who is rich in mercy,
made us alive with Christ even when we were dead in
transgressions—it is by grace you have been saved.

(Ephesians 2:3–5)

My earliest memories of God consist of a great God who loved me and everyone in the world. I remember singing, "yes, Jesus loves me for the Bible tells me so," as a child. I believed that with all my heart as a child, but I also knew of God's power. God knew everything about me and if I did anything wrong, He would get me!

I gave my life to Christ at 13 years old and tried really hard to do the right thing, but I always felt like I was struggling on a daily basis. Although I knew that God loved me, flaws and all, what I saw with my physical eyes as a teen was different. I saw Christians as perfect!

People who could quote scriptures had a special connection with God that I didn't have and that equated to "true Christianity" for me. Or as the old church ladies would say, "They were sho nuf saved." I had been in church all my life and I could barely remember John 3:16! Then there were others who looked the part, talked the talk and walked the walk. I admired them. They seemed to be totally unbothered by the

3

world. These were people who were always smiling, laughing, talking about the goodness of Jesus, and serving others. I would watch them as a teenager and wonder how they had conquered sin and were no longer tempted by anything. What was their secret? How did they get that special connection with God, that didn't come so easy for people like me? No matter how hard I tried, in my mind I just couldn't do it, so at 19 years old I gave up on being a Christian. Don't get me wrong I loved Jesus but in my warped mind, I felt that I was doing the right thing for us both. Laughable right? You can't straddle the fence with God is what the old church ladies use to say, so I stopped straddling and jumped over onto the other side.

During my years on the other side, I focused on school but there was always something missing. At times, I could sense Him calling me clearly through Kirk Franklin's music (which was the only gospel music that I would listen to) and other times I didn't hear a thing. Sometimes I would peek over the fence to see what the perfect Christians were doing and I would feel homesick. I remember deciding to go to church after a few years and I enjoyed it. On my way out the door, one of the old church ladies stopped me and said, "You know you don't have to wear so much makeup or wear your skirt so short because God loves you just the way you are." Needless to say, I didn't go back. I hopped back over the fence and as I stood there once again on the other side I told myself, "I tried."

Once I graduated from undergraduate college I set my sights on a master's degree. By this time, I was working a full-time job and going to school full time. This degree would be the peak of my life! I had worked so hard to graduate with my master's by the time I turned 31 years old and it meant the world to me. This graduation would be life changing and it would somehow make my life richer, more joyful and happy, but it didn't. My boyfriend threw me a surprise graduation party and it was great! I was being celebrated for a job well done and people seemed to be impressed but when I woke up the next day it all felt so ordinary. Everything was over and nothing had changed. I still felt like something was missing and God whispered "me".

After all those years of working and searching for my own little bit of happiness, I was right back where I was at 19 years old. At 31 years old could I do this Christian thing now? Sad to say the answer was still no. I still wasn't perfect even with two degrees I still felt like I could not be the type of Christian that God deserved. Looking back on that time in my life that wasn't the real reason. I was flat out living in sin and didn't want to stop what I was doing! Just being real. So being the sinner who desperately needed God I prayed the most selfish prayer that I had ever prayed: "God, WHEN I get married I will be settled and able to fully serve you. Please give me another chance to get myself together." Sad to say this was the first time in years that I prayed on a consistent basis mainly because I was scared. I know the nerve I had back then amazes me now but by God's grace, He kept me and soon after I got married I immediately began looking for churches. My co-worker Tamika Hyman invited me to her church and it was cool. It was bigger than what I was use to, but what caught my attention a few months later was that Kirk Franklin would be in concert at that same church: The First Baptist Church of Glenarden. I had never seen Kirk Franklin in concert and the cherry on top was the fact that the concert was free!

After the concert, an usher stopped me as I was leaving and said, "Come back and check out our worship services." She was so nice and seemed genuine. Genuine in the sense that it didn't sound like she was reading from a script. So after the concert I began attending their worship services and in April 2009, I repented, joined the First Baptist Church of Glenarden, and got baptized. That decision changed the course of my life.

I repented and instead of focusing on perfection I focused on learning all I could so that I could finally understand what God wanted from me. I attacked this journey with the same tenacity that I had when earning my degrees and the results were completely different.

Through the teachings of Pastor John K. Jenkins, Sr., Bishop T.D. Jakes, Pastor Keith Battle, Bible Institute classes, focus study classes, my family, my church family, and countless others I began to understand my new life in Christ, God's plan for my life, and the process that God uses to birth purpose.

In the next few chapters of this book I will share stories of transparency in hopes that the lessons will help new Christians understand God's divine plan and process for living a life of purpose.

PART 1

THE PLAN

A written account of intended future course of action aimed at achieving specific goal(s) within a specific timeframe. It explains in detail what needs to be done, when, how, and by whom.

CHAPTER ONE

The First Family

The Lord God said, "It is not good for the man to be alone.
I will make a helper suitable for him."

(Genesis 2:18)

In the beginning, before anything existed God had a plan. A plan that could handle the Fall of Man, a plan that would be birthed from families. The Family is important to God and is vital to our civilization. In Genesis 2:24, it says, "For this reason a man shall leave his father and his mother, and shall be joined to his wife; and they shall become one flesh." From that union, children are born and families are created providing structure for our human society.

Ask anyone to define what a family is or consists of and the terms, mother, father, grandparents, cousin, aunt, uncle, and children would be a typical response. But, is that all that a family amounts to especially today? Growing up in Georgia I routinely heard my dad refer to everyone as cuz or bruh! Even though many of those people were not close family friends some were, and they played a part in my life as a child growing up. I learned early on that family can start with blood ties but transcends based on our connection and relationships with others.

God created us for fellowship with Him and with one another starting with the family. Our horizontal relationships are just as important as our vertical relationship with the Father, Son, and the Holy Spirit.

9

All relationships are integral to God's plan!

Adam and Eve were the first examples of a family and what a family it was! From the outside, it appears that Adam and Eve had everything that they could ever want or need that is until Satan told them otherwise. It's hard to believe that with everything that Adam and Eve had that they would want for anything. They had a perfect relationship with God and all of their needs were met but they allowed Satan who was not a part of their family, to have influence in their family.

Adam was created in God's own likeness and image and Eve was formed from Adam's rib. The plan was intentional and the purpose was divine. It all made for a perfect family. Because God wants our obedience and love freely He gave us free will. The ability to choose is powerful and one choice can change the outcome of a well-intended plan and lead to consequences felt for generations to come and that's what Satan wants. His plan is simple, to steal, to kill, and destroy (John 10:10).

What does he want to destroy? Anything that God has created. But it's deeper than that. In the beginning, there was Adam and Eve and they were a part of God's family with direct access to Him. The family design was birthed out of love and fellowship, and that love and desire for fellowship has never changed. God had a plan for His first family and it started with provisions for living an abundant life. He provided Adam with a home, food, and meaningful work. Adam had fruit to eat from all kinds of trees, a home in the garden which he was responsible for taking care of (Genesis 2:9–10,15).

God loved Adam and fellowshipped with him but He also tested him when He commanded Adam that he must not eat from the tree of knowledge of good and evil because he would die (Genesis 1:16–17).

When Adam and Eve gave ear to Satan they allowed an outsider access to their soul. Satan had not provided anything to their family. He provided no fellowship, no love, and no provisions. God had provided all that was needed to nourish their body, soul, and spirit yet Satan got their time and their attention. Satan used the ole divide and conquer method when he began talking to Eve. The Bible does not provide details about why he didn't talk to Adam but what is clear is that Eve had great influence over Adam and Satan was clever enough to see that. He infiltrated God's first family and distorted God's design for the family. When Adam and Eve failed God's test they immediately died. In Romans 6:23 it says, the wages of sin is death, but the gift of God is eternal life." No, it wasn't a physical death right away but separation from God. They lost their home and all of the provisions that God had provided. Their disobedience caused them to lose the abundant life that God had freely given to them.

Satan's strategy is the same for each generation and that is to get us to take our eyes off of Jesus. Yes, he is the ruler of the world system and he appeals to the desires of the flesh in an effort to destroy our connection and relationship with Jesus Christ but it is all based on getting our attention and our focus by any means necessary.

Guard your time and your attention!

Many times we underestimate Satan failing to fully understand who he really is. In the Bible, there are over 100 verses that speak of who Satan is, his plan, and his fate. It's easy to sit back now and judge the first family and say things like, I would not have fallen for that, Eve was naïve and Adam did not provide proper leadership for his family. It's always clearer looking through the glass from the outside. But I challenge you to really see for yourself who Satan really is.

In Genesis 3:1, Satan is described as a serpent craftier than any of the other beast of the field that the Lord made. Crafty means, clever at achieving one's aim by indirect or deceitful methods. Make no mistake that Satan is clever and that he has been in the game for a long time. His end game remains the same and his mode of operation is the same, don't trust God. It's clearly revealed in Genesis 3, when Satan asks Eve, "Did God actually say, you shall not eat of any tree in the garden?" Does that sound familiar? Did God actually mean for us to tithe, isn't that Old Testament teaching? Did God really mean no sex before marriage or is that for those who are not engaged like me? Or what about this, did God really say forgive others their trespasses because my situation maybe different? Yes, I've been there even as a Christian. Asking God a question is one thing, questioning God is another.

Do your questions seek knowledge or seek to rebel?

In the beginning was the Word, and the Word was with God, and the Word was God (John 1:1). When we question the Word, we are essentially questioning God because He is the Word. Satan would have us to believe that when we question the Word that we are simply questioning something that God said. No harm in that right? Wrong! In

Philippians 4:6, we are reminded to not be anxious about anything, but in every situation, by prayer and petition, with thanksgiving, present your requests to God. This includes our questions for a quest for knowledge and understanding, not as a rebellious challenge to God's Word

The Bible also describes Satan's disguise as an angel of light (2 Corinthians 11:14). No pitchfork, no red suit, no horns. His approach appears to aid or to assist you but his intent is clear, to steal, kill, and to destroy. It may be hard to grasp all of this in the beginning of your Christian journey but the truth is this, God has you and Satan wants you back! You must be clear about this fact. 1 Peter 5:8 says, "Be sober-minded; be watchful. Your adversary the devil prowls around like a roaring lion, seeking someone to devour." The devil is on the prowl looking for you, his prey.

He found his first prey in the first family by posing a simple question to Eve, did God really mean what He said? This exchange serves as a reminder to us all that we must always be aware of who we are talking to. Little did Eve know that she was talking to Satan, the Father of lies (John 8:44).

Giving your ear grants access to your soul!

Early in my Christian journey, I didn't know how to deal with the worldly temptations that I had previously indulged in. I had been listening to Satan, the ruler of the world system for many years, now there was a new voice, the voice of God.

Hearing God and listening to Him are two different things.

It sounds logical to just listen to God but I have to admit it wasn't that easy. Even when you know that someone doesn't have your best interest you may let them talk because you have a history with that person. Satan's voice lined up with my flesh and that felt familiar. Tuning into my spirit and listening to God was new.

Learning to die to the flesh doesn't happen overnight.

I struggled for a while until I began to apply James 4:7, "Submit yourselves, then, to God. Resist the devil, and he will flee from you." I had learned to submit but it was the resisting part that I had issues with. In desperation, I opened my heart to God and asked Him to help me.

Submission and resistance only work together.

He led me back to the basics, the Lord's Prayer:

> *Our Father who art in heaven, hallowed be thy name.*
> *Thy kingdom come. Thy will be done on earth as it is in*
> *heaven. Give us this day our daily bread, and forgive us*
> *our trespasses, as we forgive those who trespass against us,*
> *and lead us not into temptation, but deliver us from evil.*
> *For thine is the kingdom, and the power, and the glory,*
> *for ever and ever. Amen.*

I had prayed this prayer as a child but now it held true meaning. Instead of reciting the prayer before bed I meditated on it day and night, repeating portions throughout the day anytime Satan came for me. That prayer and other prayers reminded me that I could not resist in my own strength, I needed my Father and His Word.

Ultimately, Satan's trick and man's disobedience led to mankind birthing sin into the world. A birthing process that would leave us dead in our sins and separated from the Father forever.

That could have been the end but because of God's love and mercy towards us, He used His original plan for the family for the purpose of saving our souls through Jesus Christ. Yes, our first family was broken but God's plan was still intact. Through murderous families, deceit, stolen identity, disobedience, and adulterous generations God would use His same divine plan to now bring forth His Son through a soiled process at an appointed time and in an appointed season. You, my friend, are no different.

Our first family was created out of love but you wouldn't know that by their actions. It's easy to get hung up on the circumstances of our birth but take a moment to think about the creation of your soul. Your mind, will, and emotions are unique to you and God took great care in creating you for a time and place such as this. Think about it, your soul could have been birthed any time and any place but God chose for your soul to enter the world during a particular date, time, season, country, and city to a certain man and woman. Before you were knitted in your mother's womb God knew you, now you have the opportunity to truly know Him.

CHAPTER TWO

Your Family

*And we know that in all things God works for the good of those
who love him, who have been called according to his purpose.*

(Romans 8:28)

Though your family may be different we all experience the
same birthing process. We are carried in the womb until our
development as an infant is complete. During that time, we are
connected to the mother through the umbilical cord. That cord was
your life source for approximately 36 weeks until it was cut upon
your entry into your family. I believe that the life of a child begins
at conception but the creation of your soul begins before the womb.
Your mother and father play a critical role in God's plan because
without them there is no life. However, your soul, the essence of who
you are as a person was created by God and He knew you then and
knows you now. In Jeremiah 1:5 it says, "Before I formed you in the
womb I knew [and] approved of you [as My chosen instrument],
and before you were born I separated and set you apart, consecrating
you; [and] I appointed you as a prophet to the nations." With that
scripture, I began to see my family with new eyes because anything
that God creates He knows.

He strategically places you with your earthly family and your
entry into that family is where life becomes very interesting. As the
saying goes, we can't choose our family. It's easy to believe that you
have the worst family that there is and that everyone else's family is
somehow better or different. Maybe you were birthed into poverty

15

and you were not nurtured or maybe you were birthed into a middle-class family with lots of love but dealt with sibling rivalry, secrets, or low self-esteem. Maybe there are so many issues regarding your family that you just can't tell it all. Our families shape our identity in this world and impact us in ways we may have never considered. We often do not even realize the full extent of those relationships and how we were affected physically, mentally, and emotionally, until years later. What I have come to realize is that no family is perfect.

I can remember as a child longing for perfection at an early age. During childhood sleepovers, I would study the dynamics of everyone's family. As I played I would sneak glances trying to process the inner workings in the homes of others. Did they eat together, did their dad ask about their day at school, did he play with them, did their dad give hugs, did their dad really see them? I was longing to see the fatherly love and so early on I began to equate love with perfection. Yes, you guessed it I had daddy issues. Although I knew I wasn't perfect, if people in my life, including family, did not live up to my idea of perfection that meant they didn't love me. And in those rare situations when I thought I had found perfection I felt like being around the source would somehow make me better because in my mind I was less than. It sounds crazy, right? But that's what Satan does best, he tricks you into believing a lie no matter how far-fetched it seems that is until you open your spiritual eyes to the truth! The truth is that the source of perfection is divine and not of this world. However, God uses our earthly pain to birth purpose.

Purpose is found in the Pain!

The smoke and mirrors trick that Satan used in the Garden of Eden was the same trick that he tried to use on me in order to steal my life and destiny! The reality is that no family is perfect but God's family plan was and still is perfect. When I rededicated my life to Christ, through much prayer and work I finally forgave my father. Oprah describes forgiveness as "giving up the hope that the past could have been any different." That definition speaks to my soul every time I read it! My lifelong struggle with perfection and feeling less than in the eyes of my father was meant to destroy me but God made it for my good (Romans 8:28). Through the pain, my heavenly Father's plan was activated and produced fruits of love and forgiveness in my life.

If you are new in the faith leave perfection to God, because we as Christians will never be perfect, but we can actively participate in God's perfect plan by producing fruit that will glorify God and fulfill His perfect plan. When I learned that lesson my perspective on being a Christian changed for the better and the chains of perfection began to fall off as I began to understand and embrace purpose over perfection.

Release Perfection and Embrace Your Purpose!

As a parent, I now understand life experiences shape us and just because we become a parent doesn't negate the fact that we are all flawed and still a work in progress. My father is a good man and a talented musician who didn't love me in the manner in which I wanted as a child. Had he known how, he would have I'm sure. However, I feel blessed to have received his gift of artistry. I remember listening to my father and other musicians practicing at our house for hours on end. Then they would leave and my father who is a self-taught musician would continue to practice alone. My father and I didn't really talk much because he was married to his music and I resented it. But this imperfect man was, in fact, speaking to me through his music. When I would close my eyes and listen close enough I could hear and feel his love through the melodies and chords he played. Unconventional? Yes, but that's how God works through imperfect people!

You see God's perfect plan is designed for imperfect people like me and you. I believe it is human nature that we all desire something greater, something beyond ourselves and many times we seek that something greater or perfection in people. After years of searching, I eventually found perfection and His name is Jesus Christ.

One of the stories in the Bible that helped at the start of my spiritual journey was the story of Joseph found in Genesis 37. Joseph, son of Jacob is, in my opinion, living the good life. He works and he is loved by his parents. However, his brothers hate him and despise his dreams. The reason for the hate doesn't matter but what is revealed once again is sin, this time in the form of deception. In this case, instead of killing Joseph his brothers sold him for twenty pieces of silver and told their father that Joseph was killed by a wild animal. Joseph like Abel was hurt by his very own family! These illustrations are not provided to fuel any negative feelings towards your family or friends or to dismiss any hurt or pain caused by your family. The story of Joseph shows me just how important and powerful the family plan is to God, how diligent Satan is in destroying God's plan, and that purpose is attached to family and to our connections with others.

Does your family have any similarities? Remember Adam and Eve were kicked out of the only home they had ever known. Then they dealt with the death of their son Abel along with the shame of being parents to the murderer of their son. Generations later we meet Jacob's family, and this time, we see sin not through murder but through deceit.

After the fall of man, sin would become a part of our human nature revealing its many faces in families everywhere. Sin does not discriminate and everyone's process begins the same way, in an imperfect family birthing imperfect people. Our Father understood the plan completely and instead of Jesus being born into a family of prestige, wealth, and influence He was born through an unlikely teenager named Mary.

Yes, our Savior's circumstances weren't ideal either. Jesus came from humble beginnings wrapped in controversy. The reality is that Jesus was born in a dirty stable to a teenage mother, who said that she was a virgin impregnated by the Holy Spirit and engaged to a man who wanted to quietly put her away. Try to imagine that!

This, my friend, was the set of circumstances that our Savior was born into. The circumstances were predestined just like ours. God's perfect plan of creation goes far beyond earthly rules or methods that we understand. For example, when we will exist, where we will live, our parents, the makeup of our body and mind are all a creation from God. Our God has planned the details of our lives according to His perfect wisdom. When I began to walk in faith knowing that He is in total control and full of mercy, my frustration ceased and peace began to set in knowing that all is really as it should be even if I didn't like it!

We are His children and He has purposely planted us in the soil of our earthly families. The soil is our environment for a time. Some people were planted in good soil based on our external perception of what good soil is while others were planted in soil depleted of nutrients needed for proper growth. Soil that may have been void of nourishment like love, safety, and structure. God knows what we are lacking and what we need to reach our full bloom and He provides all with an opportunity to be replanted into His eternal family where the soil provides all that is needed for life and growth.

CHAPTER THREE

Your Eternal Family

He predestined us for adoption to sonship through Jesus
Christ, in accordance with His pleasure and will.

(Ephesians 1:5)

After being on the other side for so many years, in April 2009, I was born into my spiritual family and adopted by my heavenly Father! As a teen I'm sure this process was explained to me but as an adult I really wanted to understand what all of this really meant. I wasn't focused on perfection anymore! God had spared my life and I was determined to learn all I could about living this new life in Christ and my new family. As the church ladies use to say, I was just glad to be in the number!

What I learned was that the moment I accepted Jesus as my Lord and Savior, repented of my sins, and asked God to live in my heart I had been born again. In 2 Corinthian 5:17, it says "Therefore, if anyone is in Christ, the new creation has come: The old has gone, the new is here." Just as children are born into their family I was born into God's spiritual family by faith and at that very moment, I became a new creation. Regardless of age or status, we are all born again as infants in Christ and just as an infant opens its eyes for the first time my spirit was awakened and my spiritual eyes were opened. As I looked around I saw other infants like me who were just happy to receive God's love but there were others who had been in the family for a while. They were established and I could tell by the way they moved through life much like the people I remembered from my childhood, they had the

Word of God in their hearts, knew how to pray, and could encourage others despite what they were going through. This time, I understood. I was a babe in Christ!

So this time I would allow myself time to be nurtured and cared for by God during my infancy stage because I desperately needed it. I basked in His love and drank milk daily. It felt so nice and for the first time in a while, I felt at peace as I was able to rest in simply knowing that God loves me and that the past was behind me. The milk nurtured me with the hope of knowing that one day the scriptures and confidence in Christ would come because my Father would teach me. He would send others to help me to learn and to grow in this new family. I had to give myself time to learn a new way of living and a new way of thinking and believe that it was possible.

This time instead of feeling intimidated I secretly knew in my heart that one day that would be me! I would be a nicer version of those old church ladies helping others.

God's process of growth is replicated throughout the universe and applies to everyone.

It's easy to get caught up in admiring the people who we believe have arrived. They seem to have it all together much like the old church ladies in my childhood. They answered the call and are walking in their gifting and fulfilling their purpose in this world. But what I had to learn was that it didn't all happen overnight. Sounds simple and logical, right? But when you've lived in the world system for so long you have to start from scratch with your thought life. The world's system does not celebrate growth but rather the pinnacle of earthly success. My perception was that overnight success was possible, but this way of thinking is very dangerous. It breeds impatience and can lead us into taking short cuts in order to get to the end result quicker. Once again this is a trick from Satan. Anytime I would attempt to take a shortcut it failed.

Worldly concepts will not work in your new Family.

What I had to learn was that our heavenly Father is more concerned with preparing our character so that when the purpose is fulfilled we are able to sustain it all. In Kirk Franklin's song "It's Not Over" the lyrics are "the prize is never greater than the lesson" and Eric Thomas says "If you're not careful, your talent will take you places that your character can't keep you." Essentially, the greater the reward the greater lesson to be learned.

Contrary to what I thought as a teen God loves us and designed the growth process for our good. In Luke 2:52, it says, "And Jesus increased in wisdom and stature, and in favour with God and man." That scripture speaks to the nature of God. He understands the importance of growth and He knows the situations and the time that is needed to mature us.

He doesn't expect us to immediately understand the plan and our purpose when we accept Jesus Christ as Lord and Savior! That is simply the first step in the journey and I've learned that you can't skip steps in this family! My initial inclination was that I would finally know my life purpose but the Holy Spirit was like not so fast Sherrell! I had to get to know my Father and through that relationship He would reveal in His perfect timing. When I look back my inclination was very selfish. I had the nerve to basically go to my Father who I claimed to love and say now tell me my life purpose without even getting to know Him. It's equivalent to an acquaintance asking you for an intimate gift without cultivating a relationship with you.

Your process and purpose are revealed through your intimate relationship with Christ.

I also found out that I was not only born again but I had been adopted as well. I tell you God covers all bases when it comes to His children! Not only does He ensure that our spirits are born again but our souls, the core of who we really are, are no longer lost. You see as a sinner we have no right to the kingdom of Heaven. No amount of good works, will-power, or positive thinking can gain us access into the kingdom. It's only through the adoption process that we gain access to our Father's kingdom and all therein.

What I didn't understand as a teen was that I was a new family member in Christ and with that newness comes a new way of thinking. My thinking never changed. I was scared of God and I did not consider myself worthy to be a part of His family. But now things were different. I understood my position in Christ was at the kindergarten level and with a humble heart, I bowed my head and opened my heart to learn.

What I learned was that I was now in a family with a perfect and loving Father and as His adopted daughter I knew I had a lot to learn not just about God the Father, the Son, and Holy Spirit but I now had new brothers and sisters who were imperfect just like me. In this family, we were all imperfect but drawing closer to our perfect Father. He was there all along waiting to welcome me into the family!

CHAPTER FOUR

A Life of Surrender

*If anyone would come after me, let him deny himself
and take up his cross daily and follow me.*

(Luke 9:23)

Surrendering to God's will isn't easy and we can't do it on our own. We must rely on Him to show us how by renewing our minds to the Word of God. We are reminded not to be anxious about anything and to present our requests to God in Philippians 4:6. When we get closer to God through meditation, prayer, praise, and worship we gain a new perspective about God's will for our life. God wants the best for us. Jeremiah 29:11 says, "For I know the plans I have for you," declares the LORD, "plans to prosper you and not to harm you, plans to give you hope and a future." The plans for prosperity and hope can only be manifested through daily surrender of our will for His will.

During those years when I was living life on the other side, I was fully engaged in the world's system. The way I thought about life, family, and success was all heavily influenced by the world system. From the outside looking in the world's system appeared to serve me well. Oh, the resume was impressive from the untrained eye. I was a hard worker, well dressed, educated, single, no children, and well-spoken. I could talk the talk and walk the walk! Yes, the world taught me to dress up the outside to mask the inside and that's just what I did for years. The world system glamorizes the external and downplays the internal that is until your life collapses and everyone tries to figure out how the woman with everything loses it all.

I was watching Dateline recently and they were telling the story about a successful businessman that had it all and lost it all. The newscaster said that the businessman's motto and keys to success were to cheat, steal, and lie if you have to but win! At first, I was taken aback a bit until I was reminded that I too lived by that motto and that I was no better than that broken businessman on the news. Had I skirted the truth at times, had I stolen time at work by working on my personal projects, had I manipulated situations for my own personal gain? Yes. This was a huge lesson for me because I had always categorized sin, therefore, I tried to categorize surrender. I had the nerve to tell the Lord that I'll surrender here, but this other area is minor and I have it under control. Yes, I tried to negotiate with God! But guess who lost? Me!

My mom had always taught me to give God the glory for all His many blessings in my life but living life on the other side awarded individuals and the term blessings didn't make much sense in a world where you work, pull yourself up by the bootstraps, and YOU make things happen. So slowly I began to believe my own made up hype. Education can be a double edge sword if you're not careful. Logic and intellect have their place but it didn't work so well in my adopted family. Don't get me wrong hard work and education has its place but having it doesn't put you on a spiritual fast track either. I learned that I had to leave my title, degrees, ego, thought life, and everything else at the door in order to live. Why? Because in 1 John 2:16, I was reminded that the desires of the flesh and the desires of the eyes and pride in possessions—is not from the Father but is from the world. This scripture sealed it for me.

We are all saved by grace through faith, not works!

What worked in my new family was faith. Initially, I had the faith of a mustard seed which was just enough to believe that Jesus died for my sins and I gladly received salvation but other than that I hadn't worked my faith muscles in quite a while. I had worked in my own strength for so long that I didn't know what it felt like to have faith in things that I couldn't see. It didn't make sense to me so I prayed and was led to Luke 9:23, "If anyone would come after me, let him deny himself and take up his cross daily and follow me." Oh, I was familiar with this scripture and it screamed surrender loud and clear As a child, I loved singing the song "I surrender all" but I had no clue what that word meant. The word surrender made me feel very uncomfortable. It was against my nature. It meant to give over, to give up, release, and let go. I asked God, *why would I want to let go of who I am? I thought that you would accept me as I am and work with me?* As quickly as I prayed and was speaking to God I was reminded that I had surrendered in the past. When I gave up on God I had actually surrendered my life to Satan!

God showed me that I had ultimately given over my control to the flesh, the world's system, pride, and the authority of it all, Satan. Yes, I had surrendered to Satan in the past and had gained nothing but emptiness inside. Although the Holy Spirit convicted me He also reminded me that with Christ all things are possible. This time I could surrender all to my creator, my Father, and my friend!

Life on the other side was a roller-coaster ride. Full of ups and downs, twists, and turns, with no hope beyond what I could do in my own strength and I, was tired. Surrendering would be difficult. I had to learn to release those things that brought me comfort and I had to learn to exercise that muscle called faith. Slowly "surrender" began to take root in various areas of my life but there were still challenges.

In my new adopted family, I would see the prayers of others being answered, and I would rejoice with them. In fact, when God answered my prayers I would be sitting high on the mountaintop fist pumping and all, but when there was silence I would apply worldly logic and send myself into a tailspin. I spent years trying to figure out what the silence meant. During the silence, I would look for signs, miracles, and wonders and beat myself up wondering what sins I had overlooked, was I reaping what I had sowed while I was on the other side, and was God displeased with me.

Just like Job, I would find myself asking God why over and over again and it got me nowhere. Eventually, I learned the lesson. I had to stop fighting God! It was like God shook me and said we're on the same team, Sherrell! So instead of focusing on the silence I learned to focus on Him, and who He was, and what He had done for me. I took my eyes off of what I wanted and began to focus on who wanted me and my attention!

Surrender and focus on the Lord!

You see surrendering to God is a daily process and the process builds our trust in Him when we don't necessarily know what the outcome will be. Surrendering our thoughts to God not only impacts us spiritually but physically as well. When I was fighting and trying to figure things out on my own I dealt with anxiety and that stress brought on my need for control, which had a negative impact on my health spiritually and physically. Ultimately, when we surrender our will for His will only then can He give us hope and a future. Yes, surrender is a battle term! God is fighting for us and He wants to capture our hearts and overtake us with His blessings but we have to throw up the white flag and surrender!

Once I surrendered I was able to experience the eternal benefits below.

Rest & Peace

I don't know about you but fighting is exhausting so when I surrender I immediately find rest in Him. There's nothing like the peace of God and physical rest. That's not a coincidence either. God designed how our bodies function and science shows that when we breathe deeply, relax, and meditate that it initiates the "Rest and Digest" response versus the "Fight or Flight" response brought on by stress. When we surrender our thoughts to Him and focus and meditate on Him and all that He is we can truly experience rest and peace that no man can provide. And our bodies can relax and function the way they were designed to function.

Reassurance

In a day and age where people are rewarded for being supermen and superwomen it's not surprising that many believe people have an "I can do it all by myself" attitude. Asking for help is sometimes viewed as a sign of weakness but 2 Corinthians 12:9 says, ". . . My grace is sufficient for you, for my power is made perfect in weakness." We have to remember not to get caught up in the day to day hustle and remember that we need Him. His power will be magnified and made perfect in our lives when we stop using willpower and our own selfish efforts to do the impossible. He's already done it! We can't save ourselves. We are weak, lacking, deficient, imperfect, and we fall short but the power of God is illuminated in our mess confirming for us and the world the unbelievable power of the Almighty God.

Trust

Lastly, when I surrender I learn to trust God more. Just like surrender trust is a process as well. I trusted God for some situations and not others. It's laughable when I think about it. I trust Him for one situation and not the other as if His power changes somehow or the ego-filled thoughts that I am somehow more capable than God of handling a particular situation. On this journey of surrender, I've learned that God has a big-picture view of every situation and that our feeble attempts to understand based on our limited intellect fail every single time. I must admit things don't make sense sometimes but I'm learning every day to trust that God has all the information: The beginning, the middle, and the end. Trust is not easy but as we renew our minds to the Word of God daily and lean not on our own understanding we can rest in the process as we learn to trust Him more.

There are many parallels between our spiritual and physical health. God wants us to meditate on those things that are good, that are pure not just for our spiritual development but He designed us as a whole being meaning that our thought life affects our body, soul, and spirit.

Please know I don't get it right all the time but now I understand that when surrender and focus collide the promises of God will explode in your life. I'm reminded of my time on the firing range when I think about this biblical principle. When I was in the Army I absolutely loved going to the firing range to qualify with my M-16. Everyone had their own lane but we were close. I could look to my right and to my left and see my fellow soldiers and I could see their targets. In the beginning, it was hard to focus that is until I was given range protocol from the non-commissioned officer (NCO) that ended up serving as a life lesson: breathe, focus, squeeze the trigger, and watch your lane! Translation, when you are led by the Spirit, His breath, He will always lead you back to Him, and He is the target!

My Prayer of Surrender

Dear God, help me to surrender it all, body, soul, and spirit. Today I dethrone myself and place you on the throne of my heart. I will follow your lead without knowing where you're sending me. I will focus on you because you are the author and finisher of my faith. I will wait for your perfect timing without knowing when it will come. In all this I patiently wait expecting a miracle without knowing how it will be provided and trust that all things are working together for my good even when I don't understand. Amen.

PART 2

THE PROCESS

A series of steps or actions taken in order to achieve a particular end.

CHAPTER FIVE

Body, Soul, & Spirit

*May God Himself, the God of peace, sanctify you through
and through. May your whole spirit, soul and body be kept
blameless at the coming of our Lord Jesus Christ.*

(1 Thessalonians 5:23)

It's easy to go about life focusing only on what we see and our physical state of being, however God's designs and plans always transcend beyond what we see and feel in the physical realm. We are all living in this physical world but experiencing life through the body, soul, and spirit. God wants us well inside and out with every part of us being complete and blameless before Christ. We are many parts, but one body (see 1 Corinthians 12:20). This divine design ensures that one part is not exalted above another, once again reaffirming the importance of relationships and family in God's plan.

Our design provides us with an intimate lesson in faith. Although we can't physically see our soul or our spirit we know that there's more to us than what we see. Think about this for a moment; the human body designed by God has 15 systems: cardiovascular, circulatory, digestive, excretory, endocrine, immune, integumentary, Lymphatic, muscular, nervous, reproductive, respiratory, skeletal, urinary, and sensory system. These intricately designed systems while functioning in the physical realm are also, connected to the unseen, our soul (mind, will, and emotions) and spirit which connects us to people in the physical realm and our Father in the spiritual realm. It's a difficult concept to grasp when I try to use my limited intellect, but in my heart I know it to be true, and that's faith! Faith to first believe in the miracle that you are!

You are God's intentional miracle!

When God created man, body, soul, and spirit He created a design that science can never replicate or duplicate on their own. In my book God was the first scientist and research and studies are constantly trying to apply logic and intellect to spiritual concepts. Illnesses and disease once thought to be brought on by genetics, nutrition, and the environment can now be connected to our emotions and our mental state of being. What does that mean? It means that Christ has set us free and those emotions, memories, and thoughts that keep us bound must be released so that we can fully receive the promises of God.

Yes, science is slowly catching up with the Word of God and we need to understand how His design works at least on a basic level. So let's take a look at emotions first. Emotions get a bad rap but they are truly a blessing from God. We were made in God's image and emotions are a part of our divine design. Our soul is comprised of our mind, will, and emotions so we are emotional beings with the capacity to feel and to express love, joy, happiness, guilt, anger, fear, etc. When our emotions are rooted in biblical truths those emotions can enhance health and healing to the body, soul, and spirit. However, when our emotions are rooted in lies, fear, sin, death etc. then those emotions can have the opposite effect in our lives.

Are your emotions rooted in the truth or lies?

Recently I was watching Bishop TD Jakes' online and he said that we should not mute our emotions but manage them. To me, that spoke volumes. Our emotions are real and they serve a purpose but, they are controllable. When emotions go unmanaged the results can impact your body, soul, and spirit. For example, unmanaged and/or suppressed anger may manifest in our physical body weakening and affecting the liver; grief may affect the lungs; worry may affect the stomach, and fear may affect the kidneys.

These emotions can affect our mental state of mind, as well as attribute to stress-related ailments such as headaches, insomnia, fatigue, as well as our spiritual walk with Christ by rendering us unable to worship in spirit and in truth, hindering our prayers, and our relationship with Christ. And here's a note for those recovering type "A" personalities like myself, research suggests that stressed-out, type "A" personalities may be at a higher risk of high blood pressure and heart problems!

But, thank God we don't have to accept that as our fate. When experiencing those emotions I've learned to submit them to the Father by opening my heart to Him and telling Him how I feel about it, and allowing Him to direct my actions through the Spirit. Ultimately, when we are led by the spirit concerning our emotions we can bear fruits of the spirits: love, joy, peace, patience, kindness, goodness, faithfulness, gentleness, self-control (Galatians 5:22–23). The fruit of the spirit glorifies God, heals us and feeds a dying world. I believe that when the world experiences spiritual fruit through our acts of kindness, love, and gentleness that it feeds their soul. The dead have nothing to offer to others who are also dead. But as the salt of the world, we offer fruit that fills the aching belly of the spirit and the living water of Jesus that quenches the insatiable thirst of the soul (Matthew 5:13).

You see when we mute or fail to manage our emotions we don't allow God to be God. We become our own God by trying to handle it in our own strength and we can't! The physical, mental, and spiritual indicators serve as divine reminders that we must cast our cares upon Him because He cares for us (1 Peter 5:7). We can also turn to our adopted brothers and sisters in Christ for help. They are a part of the family also! 1 Corinthians 12:7, says that a spiritual gift is given to each of us so that we can help each other. When I opened myself up to my new family I realized that help was available but I had to be open to receive it.

1 Corinthians 6:19–20 says, "Or do you not know that your body is a temple of the Holy Spirit within you, whom you have from God? You are not your own, for you were bought with a price. So glorify God in your body." God is concerned about every part of our being. We were brought with a price and we are His. We are His eyes, ears, hands, and feet here on earth, therefore, our sensory system plays a major role in connecting with others and the Father. Just like our emotions, we must maintain self-control regarding our senses because they facilitate what we feed our body, soul, and spirit which will be manifested through our purpose.

A key principle of keeping the body, soul, and spirit in balance with the will of the Father starts with Romans 12:2, "Don't copy the behavior and customs of this world, but let God transform you into a new person by changing the way you think. Then you will learn to know God's will for you, which is good and pleasing and perfect."

Early on I thought that renewing my mind to the Word of God simply meant to read the Bible so that's all I did for a while. Faith comes by hearing and hearing the Word of God, right? (Romans 10:17) That's correct. I was renewing my mind but the next step in the process required transformation. I had to let God transform me by giving Him access to the gateways to my soul and spirit. My eyes, ears, mouth, nose, hands, and feet had to be immersed in all things Jesus! What does that mean?

Well let me explain it this way, the Army took a quiet and shy 23-year-old woman and transformed her into a soldier. In a matter of eight weeks, I could run and march for miles, fight and defend with and without a weapon, and recite military codes at a moment's notice. How was that possible? My family was in shock and so was I. But the Army wasn't because they had done it before cycle after cycle. What was the formula? First, I voluntarily surrendered my life to the U.S. Army via an oath of enlistment. An oath is defined as a promise around something considered sacred. Affirmations are more commonplace now but just as relevant and powerful. When I gave my life to Christ I affirmed it through Romans 10:9–10:

"If you declare with your mouth, "Jesus is Lord," and believe in your heart that God raised Him from the dead, you will be saved. For it is with your heart that you believe and are justified, and it is with your mouth that you profess your faith and are saved."

When I enlisted in the U.S. Army the process of surrender went as such:

"I, Sherrell Moore, do solemnly swear (or affirm) that I will support and defend the Constitution of the United States against all enemies, foreign and domestic; that I will bear true faith and allegiance to the same; and that I will obey the orders of the President of the United States and the orders of the officers appointed over me, according to regulations and the Uniform Code of Military Justice. So help me God."

Once I surrendered my own authority over myself to the leaders over me, I was immersed into eight weeks of basic training. In those weeks, I became someone that I had never seen before, a better, stronger, more disciplined version of myself. I had a measure of faith that I would make it, but I didn't know how it was going to happen. What I learned in basic training taught me a life principle that I now use in my walk with Christ.

The impossible becomes possible during the process!

What seems impossible on the surface is possible when you are properly equipped. In a matter of weeks, I was running miles like it was nothing. I had learned how to handle an M-16 and a grenade launcher. I learned the true meaning of camaraderie when I had to lean on others to help me find my way out of the woods because I was directionally challenged. And the most valuable lesson: never leave a soldier behind.

My body was tested, my mind was challenged, and under the pressure my character oozed out!

Now don't get me wrong there were some who didn't make it. I remember those who fought the system. The Army had their physical bodies but not their minds. They would not surrender and in the end, they were discharged, leaving the same way that they had arrived.

Transformation requires your participation!

But those who made it to the end and graduated, it was evident that they had surrendered and were transformed inside and out. I had to eat, breathe, hear, see, touch, feel, and experience all things U.S. army soldier and with time I became what I saw, read, and felt! I became a soldier and the Father wants the same for us, to be transformed not by man but by the Holy Spirit!

With my new life in Christ, I am still learning how to guard my heart. In Proverbs 4:23, it says, "Above all else, guard your heart, for everything you do flows from it." What was I watching, reading, tasting, touching, walking, smelling, and thinking? I had to take an inventory of those things and submit them to the Father. In the beginning, I didn't realize that the Bible addresses all of the senses, providing guidance on what we should think, speak, see, and hear, preparing us to be sensitive to what we take in and what we put out.

He also desires all of our senses to come under the subjection of the Holy Spirit because we commune with Him through our senses.

How does God communicate? In Romans 8:5–6, it says, "Those who live according to the flesh have their minds set on what the flesh desires; but those who live in accordance with the Spirit have their minds set on what the Spirit desires. The mind governed by the flesh is death, but the mind governed by the Spirit is life and peace."

These scriptures take us back to the fruits of the spirit reminding us that our thoughts are linked to our emotions and our emotions are linked to how we experience the world. For many years, I experienced the world solely through my own selfish and fleshly motivates, rarely seeing beyond my own successes and failures. Even though I didn't pray, go to church, or read the Bible, when I was in the world I always heard God calling my name but with His gift of free will I chose not to listen for many years.

There were times when I could see Him clearly in people and circumstances, hear Him through music and nature, feel and sense His presence in certain places. God works that way. He appeals to our senses to touch our soul. Once touched I yearned to hear more and I did but not in the way that I had expected. I had unknowingly placed God in a box and expected to hear Him only through prayer but, I learned that He is ELOHIM, God Mighty Creator! As the Creator of all things, He can use all things to speak to us when we are surrendered to Him body, soul, and spirit. He uses His creation: the universe, this earth, nature, seasons, and time to speak to us. Are you listening?

Our Father is concerned about every part of our being. He reminds us that even the hairs on our head are numbered and that we are worth more than many sparrows (Luke 12:7). Our body, soul, spirit connection is the vehicle by which we experience the Father, the Son, and the Holy Spirit, our adopted family, and the world. We can't experience physical and spiritual abundance in part but in the wholeness created by the Father. When we surrender our lives to Christ our spirits are made alive and we are made whole and healed. The Holy Spirit leads, guides, fills, convicts, bears, produces, and transforms the inward parts for the fulfillment of the plan.

My Daily Surrender Affirmation

"I, [say your name], freely surrender myself to you, my Lord and Savior Jesus Christ. I surrender my mind and thoughts by fixing my thoughts on what is true, and honorable, and right, and pure, and lovely, and admirable.

I surrender to you Jesus and I die to my flesh. Teach me your ways today.

I surrender my eyes today, show me what to read and to watch. I surrender my tongue today, tell me what to say and what to eat. I surrender my ears today, tell me what I should and should not hear. I surrender my hands today, show me where I should place my hands to do kingdom work and what I should not touch. I surrender my nostrils today, as you breathed into my nostrils giving me life I will not breathe in those things that seek to steal, kill, and destroy me.

In all that I do, I do to the glory of God.

I affirm today that I will surrender, trust, and obey the Word of God, keep my eyes fixed on Jesus who is the author and finisher of my faith, and heed the Holy Spirit in all things, so help me God.

CHAPTER SIX

Who Am I Now?

Therefore, if anyone is in Christ, the new creation has come:
The old has gone, the new is here!
(2 Corinthians 5:17)

When I rededicated my life to Christ as an adult it was freeing and scary at the same time. I felt like I had been on the other side for so long and had done so much dirt that it was going to take a lifetime for those things to pass away! But God said that He had washed me clean, so I believed it! The process was complete. I was born again and adopted into my eternal family but who was I now? I most definitely didn't want to come off fake like I had it all together as a Christian nor did I want to appear as if I hadn't changed at all. In the world your identity may be determined by a number of things, like where you were born, your last name, where you attended school, what type of car you drove, the neighborhood you lived in, your education, or where you worked. All of those factors and many more play a part in how the world identifies you as a person.

I remember moving to the city for the first time and those factors became more relevant as numerous people wanted to know where I lived, what type of work I did, and what kind of car I drove. It was all very daunting but I soon learned that those factors are used by the world to determine who you are as it relates to success and status. As bad as I wanted to be somebody I never felt like somebody. My safe haven was my identity on paper. Oh, I would write, and fluff, and write some more about my accomplishments, but face to face I felt like the world saw through it all. In social settings I tried to be somebody! Some bought it and some didn't, ultimately, I didn't buy it. When I came to Christ I prayed who do you say that I am because I really don't know?

He answered with Ephesian 2:4–5, But because of His great love for us, God, who is rich in mercy, made us alive with Christ even when we were dead in transgressions—it is by grace you have been saved. This scripture reminded me that I was once dead spiritually, but now I am alive with Christ. That fact changed my perspective on my past. I didn't know who I was because I was spiritually dead! The enemy yearns to keep us in a state of death while Jesus came to give us life. Identity is defined as qualities, beliefs etc. that distinguish or identify a person. When using what I call spiritual logic over worldly logic, it makes perfect sense. Only the creator of life has the authority to say who I am because He created me!

The world does not have the authority to define your God created identity.

In Jeremiah 1:5, it says before I formed you in the womb I knew you; before you were born I set you apart. He created our original identity before we were birthed into the world, therefore, our true identity lies in the Creator.

Rick Warren says, that we are not defined by our feelings, the opinions of others, or by our circumstances. Neither are we defined by our successes or failures.

It's easy to project our experiences onto others or use our quick exchanges to define people. That's human nature right? But I'm so happy that God is not like man. As quickly as the world celebrates the wins, they are just as quick to sensationalize losses and failures, determining what events should be used to define you. But I thank God that there is no condemnation in Christ and that He is concerned about the state of our soul.

The world did not make you therefore, it can't define you!

I was a dead woman walking through life! Did you know that the word dead is defined as incapable of being stirred emotionally or intellectually, cold? This fact quickens me every time I read it. Who am I now? I am alive in Christ!

Being alive in Christ places us in a position to truly receive all that God has for us. When I truly understood and accepted His love for me, I realized that I am a friend of God! In John 15:15 (NIV), it says, "I no longer call you servants, because a servant does not know his master's business. Instead, I have called you friends, for everything that I learned from my Father I have made known to you."

I had never considered myself as God's friend before. It seemed so informal and although I was happy about it I didn't quite understand my role as His friend. You see my track record with friends was less than stellar. In the past, if my friend did something I didn't like or agreed with, they were cut off! I was self-centered, impatient, and couldn't see beyond my own desire to control my friendships. So when the going got tough, it was usually time to go, and that's how I lived most of my life. No conflict resolution, no return phone calls, and even fewer "I'm sorry". This was a new life indeed! If I didn't know how to be a good friend to the people that I saw every day how could I be a friend of God? Love.

According to the Bible, true friendship is characterized by love and not the kind of man made love that I was familiar with, the kind that is conditional. No, it's an agape love that is perfect in every way. Not only is our friendship with the Father based on love but it's an intimate relationship. Intimacy is deep, and many of us have experiences with relationships that are void of intimacy, and I was no different. I would let people get close enough to enjoy brief moments that I was able to control, yet I would remain far enough to avoid any situation that might put me in a vulnerable situation.

However, intimacy was created by God, and ultimately He wants us to experience the original intent of all that He created before it was distorted by the world. You see intimacy was modeled for us in the beginning. In John 10:30, it says that Jesus and the Father are one and in Luke 22:42, love and obedience are shown when Jesus asked if the fate of His suffering could be removed from Him. Ultimately, Jesus obeyed and said, "Ye not My will, but Yours be done."

God the Father is also God our friend.

I learned more about friendship by going back to the beginning, the book of Genesis. In chapter 22, we see a perfect example of friendship between God and Abraham. The elements of that relationship provided me with a solid foundation on which to build a new friendship with God the Father and others. Friendship God's way is built upon trust, loyalty, and obedience. On the surface trust and faith look similar but let's take it a step further. So what is faith? Even as a sinner I knew the definition of faith, the substance of things hoped for the evidence of things not seen (Hebrews 11:1). But what did it all really mean? First of all faith is a noun, something that we have, a gift from God while trust is faith in action! Many of us think we have a faith issue when we really have a trust issue.

Abraham had neither. He had faith and he exercised trust in God even during the test. All friendships are tests, and our friendship with God is no different. God told Abraham to take his only son and to go to the region of Moriah and to sacrifice him as a burnt offering (Genesis 22:1–2). Abraham was obedient as he walked out each step as instructed. He didn't delay as he got up early the next morning to move forward as instructed. He was loyal in that he didn't waiver or become distracted as he loaded his donkey preparing to move forward. Like many of us Abraham may not have understood it all but he didn't let his earthly logic deter God's plan.

When learning to trust God His plans must trump your earthly logic in every situation.

Risk is a part of trust. When Abraham took the knife to sacrifice Isaac, his only son, he made the decision to risk it all and won! Because of Abraham's obedience, Isaac, a gift from God was spared. God then shared information with Abraham, because he was someone that He could trust. He promised to bless him and to make his descendants as numerous as the stars in the sky and as the sand on the seashore (Genesis 22:15–17).

Tests are a part of God's process needed to fulfill the plan.

My growing friendship with the Father has taught me how to be a good friend to others because He provides the perfect plan for relationships that are rooted in love, and carried out through trust, obedience, and loyalty.

As the author and finisher of our faith, God created the universe and everything therein. Everything in the visible and invisible realm was birthed out of love and purpose. One of my favorite books of the

Bible has always been the book of Genesis. As a child, I loved reading the story of Adam and Eve. I was fascinated by how we all came to be but as I got older my interest faded. God rekindled that passion when I returned to Him. I was led to Ephesian 2:10. I had never read this scripture before, but when I did, my life and purpose began to truly take shape.

The scripture says, "For we are God's handiwork, created in Christ Jesus to do good works, which God prepared in advance for us to do." Wow! We were created by God's hands. This scripture really put things in perspective for me. You see God could have spoken man into existence as He did with many of His other wonderful creations but He didn't. Our Father, the original artist carefully choose specific elements to create His masterpiece, YOU! From the dust we were created to remind us of our humble beginning. And with God's breath, we were made alive and divinely connected to Him.

Man cannot give purpose to a divine design!

Even the fall of man couldn't destroy the intent of God's handiwork, because through Christ we are reconciled back to God, back to His original plan, and back to His purpose-filled work.

Psalm 139:13, says that He created our inmost being; and knitted us together once again solidifying the fact that we belong to the Father.

Did you know that you are now righteous and holy? Now this one took some time for me to grasp. Ephesians 4:24 says, put on the new man who has been created in God's image in righteousness and holiness that comes from truth. Oh, I was familiar with these terms but not in a good way. How many of you have heard, "he or she is self-righteous" or maybe you've been accused of being self-righteous. I have, and it didn't feel good. The world's system has a way of distorting the things of God by making the good seem bad and the bad good, and these terms are no different. I never wanted to be considered righteous or holy. Frankly, I thought it was unobtainable. Even people at church would quote there is none righteous, no not one (Romans 3:10).

But God showed me once again how the world had taken Godly attributes, His gifts, and distorted them and re-defined them as unobtainable. I also learned that scripture taken out of context is dangerous and confusing for new believers. But in a sense, the world was right because righteousness and holiness are not obtainable on our own. It's only possible through Him.

2 Corinthians 5:21 says, "For our sake He made Him to be sin who knew no sin, so that in Him we might become the righteousness of God." Once I read and meditated on this scripture I embraced righteousness because it's in Him that I am made right. I didn't have to work my way to righteousness thank God. It was too high a standard to reach on my own but, He never requires us to do anything alone, and holiness is no different. He says you shall be holy, for I the Lord your God am holy (Leviticus 19:2).

You, my friend, are holy because He is holy! God is holy, complete, whole, set apart, and lacking nothing! As He is separate we too shall be separate, without guilt, or sin. To the logical thinker like myself it all seems impossible or a set up for failure but it's not. Just as God's love for us washes away all of our sins our love and obedience should be the motivating factor for everything that we do. The scripture is right, none is righteous, no not one, that is when we continue to live in sin, when we fail to surrender all to God, when we want to apply worldly logic to divine principles. But when we take the time to cultivate a personal and intimate relationship with the Father above all else, then and only then will holiness become a lifestyle, as the character of God permeates every aspect of our being.

You are a mirror of God's righteousness and holiness here on earth.

I also came to understand that my entire being now belongs to Christ. Everything, body, soul, and spirit. In 1 Corinthians 3:16, it says, "Don't you know that you yourselves are God's temple and that God's Spirit dwells in your midst?" A temple is a structure reserved for religious and spiritual activities such as prayer and sacrifice. It makes perfect sense, God already said that I am holy, therefore, He should be able to dwell in me because if I am holy then that includes all of me.

God will only dwell in those who are holy.

This was another concept that I failed to grasp immediately. To be honest, I didn't feel holy at times. Many times I felt like a disappointment to God. Why was it so hard to just do the right thing? As I stood in the line to retest once again, I wondered, how David made it through. Through all of David's mistakes, he was still remembered to be a man after God's own heart. God even went as far as to say that David will do anything that I want him to do (Acts 13:22). David's story baffled me because I was using worldly logic at first. On the surface, I didn't understand how God felt about all of David's mistakes. David lusted after Bathsheba, but he loved God, David slept with another man's wife, but he loved God, David tried to cover the fact that he got Bathsheba pregnant, but he loved God. When that cover failed David had Bathsheba's husband killed, but he loved God. David's parenting skills were questionable, but he loved God.

The list goes on and on with lots of "buts". I heard in church years ago that God is a "but" God and He is! He has the ability to insert His infinite power into any situation and work it out for the good. The word "but" is used to introduce something contrasting with what has already been mentioned. God's redemptive power comes into every situation no matter how bad it is and adds truth to a situation. What I began to understand was that despite the sin, David's heart was always turned towards God.

Throughout David's life he had high and lows, victories, and defeats, but through it all, he loved God. The concept still left me scratching my head because to love is to obey Him. The Message Bible says, If you love me, show it by doing what I've told you (John 14:15). It's clear that David wasn't obedient to God in many situations, but what is clear is that he loved God and he never walked away. Sin, especially hidden sin can bring shame just like in the case of Adam and Eve which caused them to hide or to run away from God but David didn't run away from God, he ran to God.

When sin seeps into our holy temple we must run to God, repent, and ask Him to cleanse us so that He can continue to dwell in us. There is no other option! Ignoring the sin in our temples impacts our communication and our relationship with our Father, the one who resides there. God's love for us is undefinable, but our divine and holy God cannot dwell in an unholy place.

David also had faith in God and he stood on that faith even as a young shepherd boy. As a young teen, David defeated Goliath not in his own strength but through his faith in God. David is included in the "Faith Hall of Fame" (Hebrews 11) because of his faith in God.

From a worldly standpoint, it's easy to sensationalize David's story and highlight the sex, the deceit, the love child, the murder plot, and his rise and fall. That's what Hollywood movies are made of, but God!

When you love and honor God it never goes unnoticed.

David also contributed to what some consider some of the most heartfelt and powerful sections of God's Word, the book of psalms. It is the largest book in the Bible, and it's filled with songs, prayers, and beautiful poetry. David wasn't perfect, but he didn't let that stop him from pressing forward. We are all sinners saved by God's grace. So the more important question is what do you do after you've sinned? There are three parts to this answer, and they all work together meaning one can't work without the other: first we admit our sin, ask for forgiveness, and repent.

We must learn to live a life of repentance to maintain a Holy dwelling place for the Father.

In 2 Samuel 12:13, "David said to Nathan, 'I have sinned against the LORD.' And Nathan said to David, 'The LORD also has put away your sin; you shall not die.'" This moment of transparency between David and Nathan is where many of us stumble. In my desire to please God there are times when I'm ashamed or embarrassed by the way that I reacted to something that I will simply ignore it. Not in the sense that I have it all together and but in hopes that if I ignore and act like it didn't happen that God really didn't see it. Oh, the intellectual people know what I'm talking about. It's a mind game, and God doesn't play games with us. Many of us rationalize what we do or say. We do that by labeling the action and placing it in a category that our fragile little minds can handle, and the world supports this approach! We refer to the things that we do or say as "little white lies" or what I did or said didn't hurt anyone. But it did, it hurt God! We must remove the labels and the categories and call a thing a thing! That's when the light of clarity began to shine while I was waiting in the line to retest. God knows that we need Him and that we can't do anything without Him including battling sin, so He puts before us, the components of living a life of repentance and it's up us to choose. The components serve as reminders, that we can't claim freedom in Christ until we can admit those things that enslaved us in the first place.

There can be no freedom without the admission of bondage.

God knows that we're not perfect. The Word of God says that everyone has sinned and that we all fall short of God's glorious standard (Romans 3:23). However, He still wants us to keep His commandments, which demonstrates our love towards Him. But when sin hits and it will, He wants us to own up to it immediately and to ask for forgiveness. 1 John 1:9 says, "If we confess our sins, He is faithful and just and will forgive us our sins and purify us from all unrighteousness." Through forgiveness, He also purifies us from all unrighteousness repositioning us in right standing with Him. Asking for forgiveness is not just about the act being dismissed, but it's also, an opportunity to be cleansed from the residue left behind by sin.

Psalm 51 is known as the Prayer of Repentance in which David acknowledges once more what he did. You see the heart of David as he pours his heart out to God. In this prayer of repentance, he asks for forgiveness, and he repents. Our sinful nature hates repentance because it challenges our will. It doesn't feel natural especially when we fail to die to the flesh daily. I heard Pastor Keith Battle say once, I died to my flesh today, and I dethrone myself and place you on the throne of my heart. True repentance requires a heart turned towards God and the things of God. True Repentance may invoke tears and other emotions, but that's not what it's based on. It's not about just being sorry for what we did, but it's, our attitude towards the sinful act.

Sin should prompt repentance, but repentance can't wash away your love of sin!

As a teen, I remember repenting for my sins out of fear. I was sorry that God caught me and would beg for His forgiveness. I knew what I did was wrong but what was my attitude towards the sin? The Bible tells us that God hates sin because it separates us from the Father. That means our attitude towards sin should be the same as the Father. God is disgusted by sin, He hates it. In Romans 6:23, it says, "For the wages of sin is death, but the gift of God is eternal life in Christ Jesus our Lord". That's why God can't dwell in our temples when they are littered with sin. Sin brings death and God brings life. The two simply can't dwell together.

Sin separates while repentance reconnects the severed tie.

As a child, I didn't hate the sin and the sin kept coming back. We ultimately attract what we love, what we desire, and my attitude toward sin brought it back every single time.

The story of David revealed to me a man after God's heart. A man who made many mistakes that impacted lives through death and birth. But through it all, God was with him. As I stood in the line to retest, my frustration left me and my attitude changed. I made the choice, to remain in the line to retest. I would not give up. I would stand and accept God's mercy and His grace. And I embraced another opportunity to learn and to pass the test.

If are you are learning to live a life of repentance like me, I invite you to read Psalm 51. This is the prayer that David prayed after he sinned. Remember that sin separates us from the Father. Please reconcile your relationship by presenting your contrite heart to the Father through this prayer or your own prayer of repentance.

Psalm 51:1–19
A Prayer of Repentance

Have mercy on me, O God,
according to your unfailing love;
according to your great compassion
blot out my transgressions.

Wash away all my iniquity
and cleanse me from my sin.

For I know my transgressions,
and my sin is always before me.

Against you, you only, have I sinned
and done what is evil in your sight;
so you are right in your verdict
and justified when you judge.

Surely I was sinful at birth,
sinful from the time my mother conceived me.

Yet you desired faithfulness even in the womb;
you taught me wisdom in that secret place.

Cleanse me with hyssop, and I will be clean;
wash me, and I will be whiter than snow.

Let me hear joy and gladness;
let the bones you have crushed rejoice.

Hide your face from my sins
and blot out all my iniquity.

Create in me a pure heart, O God,
and renew a steadfast spirit within me.

Do not cast me from your presence
or take your Holy Spirit from me.

Restore to me the joy of your salvation
and grant me a willing spirit, to sustain me.

Then I will teach transgressors your ways,
so that sinners will turn back to you.

Deliver me from the guilt of bloodshed, O God,
you who are God my Savior,
and my tongue will sing of your righteousness.

Open my lips, Lord,
and my mouth will declare your praise.

You do not delight in sacrifice, or I would bring it;
you do not take pleasure in burnt offerings.

My sacrifice, O God, is a broken spirit;
a broken and contrite heart
you, God, will not despise.

May it please you to prosper Zion,
to build up the walls of Jerusalem.

Then you will delight in the sacrifices of the righteous,
in burnt offerings offered whole;
then bulls will be offered on your altar.

CHAPTER SEVEN

The Gardener

I am the true vine, and my Father is the gardener.
He cuts off every branch in me that bears no fruit,
while every branch that does bear fruit He prunes
so that it will be even more fruitful.
(John 15:1–2)

Parables in the Bible have always been interesting to me. It was cool listening to the stories as a child. They were entertaining and gave me hope, but I never saw a plan in it all. As a new Christian, I struggled in the beginning with this seemingly simple parables. As I searched the scriptures with focused determination to find God's plan for my life I became more and more frustrated! There were lots and lots of stories, and I had never read the Bible in its entirety before. I read the parables, but I didn't fully understand the significance of them. I felt overwhelmed! What I wouldn't give for an agenda, a syllabus, something to break down this Christian thing! I began to pray, and God answered.

In 2011, I committed to going to our Tuesday night Bible study every week. Sure that may seem like a given for some, but I had never made Bible study a priority before. It was usually an afterthought like, if I have nothing planned then I would go. So I committed to surrender my Tuesdays to the Lord. Little did I know that as I was seeking His plan for my life that I was actually in the process of the plan, and Satan knew the plan too.

The process starts with your surrender and obedience while disobedience renders delays!

The moment I surrendered, the spiritual warfare began at work. Every time I would prepare to leave work on time something would come up unexpectedly, but I pressed on remaining faithful to my commitment to God. During Bible study, I finally got the breakdown on scriptures that I was yearning for and to top it off we could ask questions at the end! I couldn't believe that I had been missing out on these study sessions. It was like school and that was something I was familiar with; so I took notes, listened, and slowly the scriptures began to make sense. But there was still something that I was wrestling with, and it was blocking my relationship with God. It caused me to withdraw and shrink. My ego was at stake, and I had to do something because the enemy was in my ear repeating, "You don't understand because you're not really His." I tried in my own strength, but I just couldn't break through.

In the end, after a few Bible studies, I swallowed my pride and said to the lady next to me, "Hi, I really enjoy the Bible studies but I'm having a hard time understanding certain scriptures. Do you have any suggestions?" Her response totally ended my struggle in this area. She shared with me how she studied using different versions of the Bible like the *New Living Translation, New International Version,* and my beloved *The Message Translation*. My world opened up from there as I began to read the scriptures in a format that I could understand. I know, it seems like a small thing but that's how the enemy works. Joyce Meyers said it best, it's the battlefield of the mind! Remember the soul is comprised of the mind, will and emotions, and Satan wants our soul!

Sure, I was aware that there were other translations out there, but there were so many that I didn't know where to start! So instead of venturing out into something new I stuck with what I was familiar with and struggled. How many of us really don't understand everything that we hear in church? How many of us go back to research and study on our own? I almost let something simple like a different way of learning hinder my blessing, but I needed help and reached out. Yes, I still had residue from the world. I wanted to be "smart" in all things God. In a twisted way, I still wanted to prove to God that I was good enough to be His. Being the melancholy person that I am I complicated things and struggled in silence for a while because of flesh. Every time I failed to surrender, I ended up in a place of frustration, and that was Satan's plan. Unfortunately, he found my Achilles heel, but the good news was that I had discovered it too. From that point on I would have to be intentional about surrendering my ego and intellect to God, minute by minute and hour by hour to prevent Satan from slithering in to talk to my ego.

Always seek understanding no matter what!

In Bible study, I began to understand concepts and principles that the enemy wanted me to remain ignorant of on my journey. I was learning the mind of Christ, and there is power in knowing and understanding divinity. God has a process for every plan, and the process clearly defines the role of God our Father, our brother Jesus, and you and me in John 15:1–2.

Jesus tells us that God our Father serves as the gardener, Jesus is the vine, and we are branches designed to bear fruit. So what does all of this mean? That's the question that I asked! A gardener is defined as someone who works in or takes care of a garden as an occupation or pastime. Gardening is also a science known as horticulture which uses science and aesthetics. And aesthetics my friend is a branch of philosophy that deals with nature, art, beauty, and taste, with the creation and appreciation of beauty! God is the original artist and in His care for us, His creation is detailed, creative, and intentional. If we go back to the beginning, we are reminded that Adam was planted in the Garden of Eden, and he worked and took care of it (Genesis 2:15). As the Holy Spirit connects the dots through the eyes of faith, we see a plan that was developed even before the fall!

God's plan transcended time, this speaks to God's omnipotence. Adam, the father of humankind, was created in God's image out of love, and made to worship, and to obey God but, he failed in the garden. But in God's divine plan He didn't create another, He sent His son to save and to right Adam's wrong. And once again in the garden we see a reflection of Adam's sin through the suffering of Jesus in the garden. The life, death, and resurrection of Jesus completed God's plan, and now we reap the benefits of that Holy plan. As Jesus hung His head and died, He donned a crown of twisted thorny branches on His head taking full responsibility for our disobedience and brokenness.

In the garden all is visible to the gardener.

That circle of thorns represents the severed connection that was made whole and holy once again.

*God's plans are full of divine connections
visible only in the spirit.*

As our vine, Jesus is essentially our life support system. In Him we have brotherly support, we have life, and we can bear fruit which is what God wanted all along.

I was never one for memorizing scriptures but early on in my journey, I decided to enroll in a discipleship program at my church to further develop my relationship with Christ. It was in the program that I intentionally began to memorize scriptures and John 15: 1–2, was one of the first ones that I memorized. I was excited because this was going to be just like school. I crushed school and this would be no different!

But in the deep and secret places of my heart, it really wasn't for God. I wanted to fast track to this super Christian status. You see in the beginning, God rescued me and I was thankful. However, after some time, I determined that I wasn't progressing fast enough as I looked around at others. Comparisons was my first mistake.

The root of perfection is comparison yielding sorrow.

But this program would be my fast track to equal status with my peers. I loved collecting anything with a seal, and this was no different. Little did I know that this would be the first program that I would fail to complete.

In the beginning, I soared and the success slowly began to feed my ego again. It felt great. I was completing my homework on time, memorizing scriptures, and gaining knowledge. Satan was talking and I was talking right back. In military terms, "communications" had been established, and before I knew it, I was back on this self-absorbing ride to prove that I was somebody. This program was designed to cultivate my relationship with the Father, so when it came to the transparent group sessions, I refused to do the work. What did sharing my business with strangers have to do with my rise to Christian stardom! I needed that certificate, and I was determined to get it! But I didn't get it because I failed the quizzes and the test. Confused? Yeah, so was I in the beginning. Let me explain, I passed all of my program requirements and was close to graduating before I failed God's requirements. In the midst of a transparent group session, someone challenged me about a personal matter, and I flipped out. Anger oozed from unmanaged emotions and in a fit of rage, I left the program. Yes, a few months shy of completion I quit. Sound familiar? For months I was angry at those who had challenged me and although my facilitator reached out to me many times I refused to engage. After a few months, I opened my heart to God and showed Him the wound. Like a child with their parent, I pointed to the wound and said see daddy the church did that, and His response was no you did that! Then He revealed the answers to the quizzes and to the test that I had failed.

Even kingdom work requires a heart check!

To my surprise, the quizzes and the test had the same answer: Apart from me, you can do nothing. It was that simple. As I began to dissect the situation, I realized that once again Satan went right to my Achilles heel, and, this time, he had won. Despite my intellect, I wasn't going to get that certificate, because, without Him there is no fruit. He was not going to reward my selfish motives, but because of His mercy, I got a retest. I got a retest!!

There would be more quizzes, tests, and retests for me but I learned a valuable lesson from the whole situation. I must check my motives even in church! It all felt like such a setback. I was embarrassed and disappointed, but in my brokenness, I drew closer to God. And like the caring Father that He is, I was forgiven and given an opportunity to start again.

His light shines through the cracks of our soul revealing the true heart of a man.

I was watching the Oprah show one day, and she said something that was so simple, yet it cut straight to the core of my wounds. In her 25 years of lessons learned, she said, that every person that we will ever meet shares that common desire: They want to know, "Do you see me? Do you hear me? Does what I say mean anything to you?" That was it! Although I had forgiven my father, the wound had not healed because I never identified that there was a wound! You see that situation had to happen in order for me to finally be transparent with myself and God before I could be transparent with anyone else.

I realized that I was yelling to anyone that would listen: I'm here and do I matter? The world taught me the sure fire way to gain attention and credibility were through education. I didn't have a lot of material things, but I felt that I could fight with something that we all have; our minds. I had determination and I always finished what I started that is until I flipped out in the church program! All in all the first scripture that I learned in the program was the very same scripture that would set the foundation for my test. Apart from Him, we can do nothing, and I can personally attest through that experience, as well as others, that we must stay connected to the vine at all times and in all things!

Tests are a part of God's plan but so is mercy.

Because of God's love for us and our connection to the vine, He holds the sole responsibility for pruning us to yield more fruit. Pruning is a purification process that is painful for the flesh but life giving to the soul. This process is essential for our spiritual growth and development as long as we are living and breathing on this earth. The Master Gardener with infinite wisdom and knowledge selectively cuts and removes things in us that are dead and diseased so that much fruit can be produced. I used that word "much" intentionally because those of us who are connected to the vine and abide in Christ are fruit producers but much fruit only comes through pruning.

Pruning is death to the flesh and life to the soul!

In John 15:4 says, "Remain in me, as I also remain in you." When we are connected and abide, we become subject to the purification process reserved for His chosen people, the imperfect people. Purification is the result of the pruning process which frees us from things that pollute and contaminate us. In order for God to cultivate the fruits of the Spirit in us, we must abide in the Father, stay connected, and remain surrendered, body, soul, and spirit throughout the process.

Once I understood this process, I cried! Yes, I literally cried. I felt overwhelmed. This process was going to be intense, cutting and separating, definitely weren't words that I was praising God about! In Hebrews 4:12, it says, "For the Word of God is quick, and powerful, and sharper than a two-edged sword, piercing even to the diving asunder of the soul and spirit, and of the joints and marrow, and is a discerner of the thoughts and intents of the heart."

Painful, stressful, and impossible were some of the words that came to mind as I prayed about this process. This pruning process wasn't a day surgery kind of situation! No, this was going to be major surgery with no anesthesia! On the table, my Master cut me. The Word was sharp, and the cut was deep, and precise. With eyes wide open I saw bitterness leaking from my heart and pride oozed from my soul. I saw fruit too, but there wasn't a lot of it because old things and dead things were in the way. I began to cry, not from the pain, but because He found it!

He had found those things that I had hidden, so deep that there was no way anyone could reach them that is except the Father. There were so many things that were hidden so after a while I braced for the next cut, but it didn't happen. I had made it through the surgery! It was over!

The Gardener refines and cleanses for more growth.

The temporary pain from the cuts faded as life filled my heart and soul. More fruit was forming inside, and I felt it! The contaminated and stubborn areas had been purified, by the Word and the Holy Spirit. As I rested in the recovery room, I felt light, I felt free, and alive. The Fruit was coming forth. It was worth it! I made it through, and the Holy Spirit comforted me. After a few days of recovery, I was released, but not before the Father handed me a note, saying, "See you soon Daughter. You have more surgeries scheduled. I love you." Say what now?

CHAPTER EIGHT

Gifts & Talents

*There are different kinds of gifts, but the same Spirit
distributes them. There are different kinds of service, but the
same Lord. There are different kinds of working, but in all
of them and in everyone it is the same God at work.*

(1 Corinthians 12:4–6)

God has blessed all of us with gifts, talents, and abilities. No one
is left out no matter how ordinary you may feel. I had always
heard about spiritual gifts, but I didn't really understand how the gifts
worked. Growing up. I was always attracted to the arts. As a child, I
was a cheerleader, ran track, took ballet classes, and sang in chorus in
school. But did that mean that I was in the wrong profession since I
wasn't a professional singer, dancer, or track star? I wasn't sure.

I came to God because I was empty and wanted to be made whole
and complete. I was also, searching for my purpose. What was I put
on this earth to do? Was I in the wrong job? I wasn't even sure about
these gifts that everybody kept talking about. It all seemed divine but,
I couldn't grasp what it all meant, so I took a spiritual gifts class at my
church. Through that class and my own personal studies, I learned
about the gifts!

Spiritual gifts are endowments or supernatural graces which all
Christians need to fulfill the mission of the church. In 1 Corinthians
12, we learn more about the Gift Giver and the purpose of the gifts.
Specifically, the gifts are given to God's people by the Holy Spirit.
Why? To equip His people for works of service, so that the body of
Christ may be built up (see Ephesians 4:12).

Biblical References to Spiritual Gifts:

- Romans 12:6–8
- 1 Corinthians 12:4–11, 28–31
- Ephesians 4:7–13
- 1 Peter 4:10

God determines all endowments, and the beauty of it all is that no gift is greater than the other. They are all designed to complement each other and to build up the kingdom of God. Through God's divine wisdom He determined which Spiritual gifts you would receive from the Holy Spirit and that decision is a perfect fit for you!

Your Spiritual gifts and natural talents become clear while serving others.

Natural talent is given by God as well, but it's not a spiritual gift. Natural talents are skills and abilities, like athletic ability, musical ability, intellect, artistic aptitude etc. The list goes on and on. So what's the difference? We all have natural talent, but only God's people receive Spiritual gifts. As God's children, we serve as stewards of our gifts and talents as we use them to glorify God. In 1 Peter 4:10, it says, "Each of you should use whatever gift you have received to serve others, as faithful stewards of God's grace in its various forms."

The parable of the talents in Matthew 25:14 is a wonderful illustration of stewardship. In the parable, three men are given talents. The one that was given five talents gained five more, the one that was given two gained two more, but the one that was given one simply buried it and gained nothing. At the heart of stewardship is obedience. I had many retests in this lesson! Those times when I failed to surrender all to God, I would treat His precious gifts as my own! I mean they felt like mine, they looked like mine, people acted like they were mine, but they weren't.

I passed the test when God reminded me that apart from Him I can do nothing (John 15:15). Here we go again I thought that I had learned this lesson, but before I could beat myself up about the failure the Holy Spirit helped me to understand that life is a journey and that I had to learn to live a life of surrender and a life of repentance because there would be more failures and more retests. I couldn't wallow, I had to learn the lesson, repent and pray.

We are entrusted to manage the gifts and talents that God owns!

As His child, He entrusts us to manage the gifts and talents that will ultimately glorify Him. As we honor God with our obedience by giving Him full authority over all that He has given to us then and only then can they operate at their optimum heavenly level. Spiritual gifts and talents rooted in human logic produce no gains and the water from our feeble intellect provides artificial nourishment leaving our gifts and talents dehydrated and inoperable.

Heavenly gifts won't operate at full capacity without an active connection to the gift giver!

When we give and sow good things, our lives along with our gifts and talents benefit and flow. But, it all starts with our thought life. From our thoughts seeds are formed, and seeds carry life and the potential for growth if sown properly. The manifestation of those thoughts then flows from our lips. Just like seeds our tongue carries life and death (Proverbs 18:21). In Genesis, God said, let there be light and there was light, establishing heaven's first order, that words hold power! The words we speak carry a frequency of death or life into the atmosphere. Therefore, we must guard our hearts from where the issues of life flow.

Sowing is the first step in reaping a harvest.

As easy as it may sound being intentional in our sowing can be difficult. You may want to invest in your education for a better job or forgive and reconnect with a family member, but you're waiting for the right time. We can't wait for the right time to sow even when it seems difficult. There is no perfect time to sow God's Word because the enemy's goal is for you to never sow the seed! We must never forget the enemy's goal is to block life. Sow through the tears, sow even in the pain, sow good seed no matter what!

The enemy doesn't care about the dream, he seeks to block its manifestation!

As I challenge you, I reflect on how I responded when God presented me with *"Sow no matter what challenge"* in 2011. If you haven't participated in this challenge, it's coming. I had always given when I was in church, but I was never a consistent tither. So when I started attending Bible study regularly Pastor Jenkins devoted several Bible studies to tithing, and I began to understand what it all meant. It wasn't necessarily a sacrifice as I once thought but it was based on obedience. Logically, it didn't sound quite right but spiritually it made perfect sense. It wasn't about being stupid and naïve to give money to support the church and the pastor. That's what me and my friends use to say out in the world. I would say things like "I'll give but I ain't giving all my money to take care of a family I don't even know". It's funny now but being in the world back then I didn't understand spiritual concepts and principles and I wasn't supposed to. Once I understood, I put the principle to the test and began to tithe and give offerings regularly. Everything was working well until talk of sequestration began to buzz in the D.C area. Immediately, the enemy came to steal the Word from my heart by offering me fear. He said you know you need to stop tithing Sherrell because your job is in jeopardy. But I didn't take the bait.

But the enemy is persistent. Remember he had me once and he wanted me back so like an old boyfriend he approached me from a different angle. In a voice of concern, he said that he understood my commitment. That got me to turn my head. Now he had my attention, he goes on to say that God loved me. He was right, so now I'm wondering was there another way. Then the enemy proposes just put your tithes and offering on hold until things are worked out. Now when he said that I pondered it. No one would know, and if I can be honest I had never been in this type of situation before. Wouldn't God understand? I believe what I had been learning in church, but it was all so new. God had to come through because I knew this world's system and as secure as the federal government seemed things were changing, and I had to come up with a plan to protect my family and our finances. Desperate times called for desperate measures, is what my ego said.

The enemy comes with a mixture of truth and lies to confuse the flesh but he can never confuse the spirit!

I pondered for a moment and cried out to God. I really wanted to be obedient, but my ego and pride were yelling at me by this point. But God spoke and silenced all the voices, and He simply said, do you trust me? On my knees, scared, and crying, I said yes, and that was it. When I got up, I committed to sowing through the pain with a cheerful heart. What the enemy proposed wasn't right. It sounded great to my flesh, but my spirit was not deceived. God already knew about my job situation and the Word tells me that God can't go against His Word. Now don't get me wrong there would be more tears and nights on bended knees. The agency that I worked for at the time even sent us all home for a week with no pay. I remained obedient and stood and cried.

Months later as quickly as things seemed to be falling apart the agency that I worked for paid us all for the time we lost. In 2012, I received cash awards, time-off awards, and a prestigious agency award. God restored all that I lost and more. That challenge lasted for a year. I had never been challenged in my finances before, and I'm just so glad that when it happened that I was saved. I can only imagine what the old me would have done. But the lesson that I would learn over and over again in other areas of my life was that you can't separate God's love from obedience. I will never forget that year and that time in my life because in my desperation I drew closer to the love of my life and He drew closer to me.

Even as a backslider I knew of the sowing and reaping principle but it was from a position of despair. Let me explain. When I was out in the world, I would rejoice selfishly when I was blessed. I would think oh, maybe I'm not that bad! But as soon as something bad would happen I would hear the echoes of the old church ladies saying "See baby, you're reaping what you sowed." I was so confused out there in the world! I wasn't with God, but I was always aware of His presence in the world. I was torn, for a long time. You see I accepted the bad when it happened because I wasn't good and I knew it. I was mean to people, I had no patience, and disposed of people when things didn't go my way, so of course I had to accept the bad.

But when I returned to the Father, I realized that I still had that same old mindset. Now that I was doing kingdom work, I didn't know how to expect that something good would happen. It sounds silly, but it took a while to learn that when I sow forgiveness, love, joy, and kindness that I will reap an abundant harvest of those seeds. Many of us put work into planting our seeds but the seeds won't grow because we don't expect them to. It's a simple concept but missed by many. Sowing starts the harvest process, but expectation nurtures it. We must have the Word of God in our hearts, and then we must release expectancy through faith. It starts by speaking the Word of God over our seeds. Luke 6:38 says, "Give, and it will be given to you. A good measure, pressed down, shaken together and running over, will be poured into your lap. For with the measure you use, it will be measured to you."

Sowing starts the harvest process but expectation nurtures it!

When we plant seeds, we must then position ourselves by standing on the Word of God as we wait patiently to receive what God promised. What does standing on God's Word mean? It means we stand and pray in faith knowing that the good seeds that we planted will reap a harvest. It means in this portion of our lesson we will be exercising our faith muscles, and it will be difficult. The seed is planted and surrounded by darkness. There is no light, but there is nourishment provided by your words through faith. In time, the seed will produce the same in kind as we sowed.

> *Sow a thought, reap an act;*
> *Sow an act, reap a habit;*
> *Sow a habit, reap a character;*
> *Sow a character, reap a destiny.*
> Ralph Waldo Emerson

In the beginning of this chapter, you will notice that I said that "I learned about gifts. I didn't rattle off my gifts and talents because God showed me that it wasn't important. Now don't get me wrong. I see the gifts at work when I'm serving, but the importance isn't "I know I have this and that gift" but in the fact that God will equip me with whatever I need to accomplish His good work! Our spiritual gifts shouldn't box us into a particular category as we are all called to the Great Commission! Yes, even shy people like myself.

I learned that regardless of the gifts and talents, we are all called to fulfill the Great Commission. Matthew 28: 18–20, "Then Jesus came to them and said, "All authority in heaven and on earth has been given to me. Therefore go and make disciples of all nations, baptizing them in the name of the Father and of the Son and of the Holy Spirit, and teaching them to obey everything I have commanded you. And surely I am with you always, to the very end of the age."

When I got a better understanding of the Great Commission, I immediately started making excuses. I said things like well God I'm shy and from what I understand you made me this way so did you really mean everyone? After His resounding yes I later learned that the Great Commission looks different for everyone. To me, it initially looked like street witnessing, and I cringed every time I thought about it, not to mention, how was I going to make disciples out of anyone when I was still so jacked up? I'm still trying to get my life straight! But once again, I was reminded that He will equip me! Hebrews 13:21 says, "equip you with everything good for doing His will, and may He work in us what is pleasing to Him, through Jesus Christ, to whom be glory for ever and ever. Amen."

We are never ill-equipped to carry out God's will.

Just like in the Garden of Eden God prepared everything that Adam would need to accomplish His will, and you and I are no different. We have the gifts and talents; what we lack sometimes is the faith to believe in what God has placed in us because we don't see it for ourselves. But we must see what God sees in us through the eyes of faith! I know it's hard because I still struggle in this area but as always I must lay aside human logic for spiritual logic concerning the supernatural. God specializes in doing the impossible so that He can get the glory. Yes, people will doubt your credentials and question your Christianity, but I'm here to tell you it doesn't matter what people say. Remember don't allow people to label you because your true identity has been established by God. The world doesn't understand the ways of God so don't expect them to. In fact, some of the saints don't either because of their own experiences. As the old church ladies would say, "in everything get an understanding for yourself!"

So how do you carry out the Great Commission? Just let the Holy Spirit flow through you. He will use your gifts and talents to win souls. In fact, you may win a soul to Christ or plant a seed through prayer, teaching, or encouragement. Whatever industry or platform you may or may not have there is always an opportunity to connect with people's hearts. Maybe you offer them a helping hand, or share your testimony through casual conversation. It's really not as formal as I thought in the beginning. We simply start by feeding the hunger that we once had by offering them spiritual fruit which consists of love, joy, peace, forbearance, kindness, goodness, faithfulness, gentleness, and self-control. Against such things; there is no law (Galatians 5:22–23). Once you feed someone's initial hunger they are more open to receive and may engage in conversation or possibly a relationship with the one who feeds them just like Christ fed us. Then at the leading of the Holy Spirit simply share your testimony. When I learned this simple concept many things came together for me.

Lessons Learned

- All things are given by God for us to manage. The world would have us to believe otherwise.
- My life including my gifts and talents are to be used for the Great Commission in a manner that is unique to me.
- Purpose is a journey, not a destination.
- When we fail to manage properly the things that God has given us we cannot expect a harvest.
- Love and obedience work hand in hand.

CHAPTER NINE

Understanding Seasons & Time

*There is a time for everything, and a season
for every activity under the heavens.*
(Ecclesiastes 3:1)

I never paid too much attention to seasons until I became an adult. Being a native of Georgia, I was accustom to shorts in the winter and shorts in summer and I loved it. I could never imagine, actually living in a place like D.C. I had no desire to experience snow, all weather gear, or anything associated with cold weather. But I was here, and I began to wonder what it all meant. God knew me, and I was built for sun, fun, and sand so why was I here? Oh, my husband is a Washingtonian, that's right. In the beginning, I would fight the winter subconsciously by refusing to wear winter clothes until I absolutely had to, holding onto my little bit of sunshine.

A cycle began to form, and before I knew it each September, depression would set in like clockwork. My life would feel dried up, and all I wanted to do was stay in the house and sleep. I hated the snow, dreaded the holidays, and would count the days until spring. In 2015, I had a breakthrough when I journaled my thoughts after much prayer and meditation.

God showed me that seasons serve a purpose no matter how much I dislike them. You see, we serve an intentional God who creates everything with purpose and order. In Genesis, God created all of creation in a particular order, and He chose to do it in six days and rested on the seventh day. In all of His power and glory, God rested, not because He had to, but He was providing us with the perfect plan to model as we sow, work, and rest. He created the sun, moon, and stars on the fourth day, blessing us with time and seasons. Isn't it interesting that we have four seasons when they were created on the fourth day? God simply amazes me with His detail, order, and timing.

God's divine order is demonstrated through time and seasons. In Genesis 1:14, God said, "Let there be lights in the vault of the sky to separate the day from the night, and let them serve as signs to mark sacred times, and days and years." And in Genesis 8:22, it says as long as the earth endures, seedtime and harvest, cold, and heat, summer, and winter, day, and night will never cease. These indicators reaffirm God's wisdom, power, and control over all things. While this order is clearly demonstrated in nature, we also, experience this order in our lives through seedtime and harvest.

God showed me that my mindset was out of season. I was so focused on what I was losing that I failed to understand the purpose for every time and season. It became clearer when God led me to Ecclesiastes 3:1, "There is a time for everything, and a season for every activity under the heavens." Left to my own devices, I would bask in the warmth of the sun and live out all of my days in one season missing out on the lessons and the blessings from three other important seasons.

God being the first scientist shows us through the beauty of His creation the purpose for seasons and time. You see, seasons have a beginning and an ending. They were never meant to last forever. They all complement each other preparing us for the next. God's master plan is perfect! To be all that He calls us to be God blesses us with seasons and time which we need in order to die to self, grow, and to mature in our walk with Christ.

Seasons produce faith and trust, and without them the fullness of our greatest gift, life won't be realized. Some seasons and time are easy breezy while others have more pressure associated with them but God uses all things even the pressure to bring out the best in us. Even in nature, there is an element of pressure that is needed to maintain balance. God as the master artist knows how much time, pressure, and heat that is needed to reveal the brilliance within. It can't come forth any other way. Even in your state of brilliance, the Father must also cut and polish you ensuring that the good work that He began will be carried out to the day of completion (Philippians 1:6). Each part of the process is designed to bring forth the excellence within. God knows the beauty and sees the beauty in each of us but it can't come forth through stagnation but through a state of change.

Seasons

Color and new life comes forth in the spring. Colors paint nature and the sky as an increase of energy begins to flow into the atmosphere. Seeds that were sown rise up and begin to grow. You see the beginning stages of what's to come. The days become longer preparing us for more daylight to work in the next season. Branches that were once bare now bear fruit, as all of God's creation receives sun and rain for optimum growth. Creatures come out of hibernation and begin to work. The earth and everything in the earth is growing. It's a joyous time, and if you think about your own life, I'm sure that you can recall your spiritual spring seasons. When I rededicated my life to Christ, it was spring 2009. I was excited I had just celebrated Good Friday and Resurrection Sunday, and I felt like my best years were ahead of me. I was full of energy and on fire for God! I saw abundance all around, and it felt surreal. I wanted to hold onto that feeling forever. The joy I felt was great, but I now know that emotions can't sustain us spiritually.

Spring is marked by the abundance seen through all of God's creation.

Summer is similar to spring but instead of the beginning stages we see the fullness of abundance all around. There's less rain because everything is in full bloom. Because the soil is ripe and the days are long, this is the time to work. This is seedtime. It's not by happenstance that there is an increase in family, business, and social functions in the summer. This is the time to connect, to form partnerships, and collaborate. Our Father wants us in fellowship with one another, regardless of the season, so we must take advantage of every season where connecting is concerned. In the summer season, it's hot and the heat can be draining while we work. The rain is distant but when it comes there's a refreshing experience by all of God's creation as He cools the land and our situations. As much as I love summer I routinely pray for God to send His rain.

During this time, we must be careful to not let work consume us. I say that because it happened to me. I was so excited about being saved and working in the church that I was there all the time. But God wants us to have balance, and as Pastor Jenkins says, ministry starts at home. God doesn't want us to neglect our families for the church nor the church for our families. Everything has its proper time and place so we must be led by the Holy Spirit in all things even if it's kingdom work.

The summer season is also the hottest of all the seasons and the optimum time for pruning, refining, and purifying. This process must occur before the fall or the harvest season.

Summer is marked by pruning and purifying.

In the fall the sun moves lower in the sky, decreasing the light and warmth that we grew accustomed to in the summer. God gently prepares us for the darkness to come in the winter season. Vibrant colors are replaced by subtle fall colors and growing season ends. This is the time to reap your harvest and prepare for winter. It is also, a time of letting go and reflecting. You see the beginning stages of winter as the temperature drops and the leaves wave goodbye. Branches that were once plentiful are now bare and all of God's creation retrieve their harvest in preparation for the winter. The earth and everything in the earth is preparing, reflecting, and slowing down.

We must slowdown in order to reflect and to prepare.

I've often read that fall is regarded as a melancholy time, and I couldn't agree more. For me, it's a time to say goodbye to the summer. I don't fight it anymore as I give myself time to slowly accept that I will see summer again real soon. I savor the summer season while I prepare my mind for the winter season in the fall.

"Autumn . . . the year's last, loveliest smile."
William Cullen Bryant

In this season, school is back in session and work resumes. It may even feel like summer as far as work is concerned, but that's out of order. Anytime we try to prolong or shorten a season we are basically saying that we don't trust God's order and timing of things. It's an act of disobedience and that's what I was doing when I would boldly wear tank tops and shorts in the fall when it was past the summer season. It was an act of rebellion that I'm not proud of but thank God for mercy and understanding.

Our thoughts, words, and actions can speak obedience or disobedience, loyalty or rebellion.

During this season, you may begin to feel spiritually dry. The energy may be different as there's a subtle shift towards stillness. It's a time of letting go. Some lose loved ones and some reflect on life and lives lost. Like the other seasons, the fall season is purposeful in a different way. This is the time to rekindle and reconnect with our Father, especially if you were a workaholic in the summer like me and lacked balance. Remember He will never leave nor forsake us. He's always there waiting.

This is the time to snuggle up with God the Father, Son, and the Holy Spirit to reminisce, to love on one another, and prepare. God has plans to prosper us and to give us a hope and a future (Jeremiah 29:11). Our own plans are common, at best but God sees the beginning, middle, and the end!

Our plans are based upon limited information while God's plans have all the information needed to accomplish good work!

In the winter all color is erased and white illuminates. In this season the days are short and the temperatures are low. The growth season is on hiatus, and the trees are bare. Life may be hard to see as this is the time to rebuild resources. The earth is marked by darkness, cold, snow, and ice. Some animals migrate to a warmer climate while others hibernate living upon the stored harvest that was gathered. During this time, God may feel distant, but He is still there. During this season, it's easy to feel abandoned by God. The coldness in the atmosphere can leave your spirit chilled to the bone. But as I mentioned before we can't rely on our emotions. Our emotions are fickle therefore we must stand on the Word of God while holding onto our faith. You're still a friend of God, He's just not talking at the moment. His love never changes and neither should you.

God is not moved by our emotions but by our faith!

This was a hard lesson for me to learn in the beginning of my journey because I was coming off of a spiritual high and didn't understand why it couldn't last forever! I thought there was something wrong with me, but that's a trick of the enemy. He plays on our emotions which we must manage. Don't let the spiritual winter season get you down. Take the time to rebuild and utilize your resources to reaffirm your relationship with Christ during this season which is only for a specific period of time.

The seasons and their description, are not set in stone. The descriptions were provided by context, to our spiritual seasons. Ultimately, the seasons and time teach us that God always provides a preparatory season in which to prepare for the next. As God moves us through different seasons in our lives, we must ask the Holy Spirit to help us to discern what season and time we are in. Once we discern that season, we must touch and submit to His will, and surrender.

Do you find it hard to change your mindset, like me? Do you find yourself stuck year after year, longing to stay in that sweet spot? If that's you let's pray.

A Prayer for Embracing Change

Father, you designed each season to cultivate the best in me. As my Father, you know what's best for me, and I trust you. I will not allow my past to hinder my future as I now reaffirm my commitment to you and your plan. I will greet each season with gladness as I look for opportunities to grow mentally, physically, and spiritually. Through the seasons, I will remain in you and you in me.

Because you love me, I know that you will prune and purify me so that I may bear more fruit in due season. Though the pruning and purification may be difficult, I surrender daily to the process. I trust and believe that you know what's best for me, whatever season you have me in. I pray this prayer by faith in the name of Jesus. Amen.

CHAPTER TEN

Transparency in Christ

Then the eyes of both of them were opened, and they realized they were naked; so they sewed fig leaves together and made coverings for themselves. He answered, "I heard you in the garden, and I was afraid because I was naked; so I hid."

(Genesis 3:7, 10)

When I gave my life to Christ in 2009, I didn't know what to expect. He met me in my desperation and promised to love me and to never leave me. With limited information, I took His hand and began to walk not knowing how drastically my life would change. No matter how long you've been out in the world or what you did while you were out there God still wants you. He called me for years, and I tuned out His voice hoping that He would stop. But He never did. You know that voice? It's the voice of God telling you that there is a better way to live and that He holds the answer.

I always knew that He was the answer, but fear had a tight grip on me because of what I would have to give up. I thought that being a Christian would be boring and a life filled with a bunch of "you can't . . ." That's the lie that the enemy told me and I believed it for many years. I really believed that I would be missing out on life by living for God; not fully understanding that there is no life without Him.

The life we have in Christ is vibrant and visible. We are the light in a dark and fallen world. Transparency allows God's light to shine through us so the world may see. People are naturally drawn to light, but they can't see it through a covering. God's original design was built on transparency. He wants us to freely open and give our hearts to Him. When we come to Christ He doesn't force us to do anything. We still have free will to choose.

Before sin covered the earth, Adam and Eve were naked in the garden. God saw them and they saw God. This was God's original design. There was nothing to hide because God loved man and man loved God. But, the fall of man ushered in guilt and shame, so Adam and Eve covered themselves and hid from God. Adam and Eve covered themselves from God, and from one another. Born into sin our flesh is wired to cover and to hide from God. This sometimes unconscious behavior has survived throughout the ages. As we are born into sin, the world's system preps us for covering at a young age. Many of us are taught to mute or to cover our emotions, cover what we dream, to do out of fear, cover a broken heart with drugs, cover insecurities with unhealthy relationships. The list goes on and on, so with each generation more and more layers are added to the covering. In our meager attempts to cover ourselves, we also try to hide from God, not fully understanding His omnipresence in every area of our lives.

My covering has many layers as well, but with each test and every surrender, I submit and allow God to remove the layers. They don't come off easily sometimes therefore, some of the layers have to be cut off as opposed to simply removing them. Eventually, the final layer will be removed so that God and others can see me and the light that shines through me.

They triumphed over him
by the blood of the Lamb
and by the word of their testimony;
(Revelation 12:11)

About the Author

Sherrell Moore-Tucker is an author, speaker, Mind-Body Wellness Advocate and creator of Faith & Flow Yoga a practice designed to meet the needs of those desiring a Christ-centered yoga practice. Faith & Flow Yoga specializes in Faith-Based Yoga which is an intentional practice of connecting our entire being, body, mind, and spirit with God. This is NOT a traditional yoga class. Under the guidance of the Holy Spirit, Sherrell facilitates a worship experience; allowing pace and time for each person to experience God for his/herself on the mat. She uses biblical principles like surrender, transformation and discipline as the building blocks of faith ultimately enhancing spiritual and physical growth and development through Christ.

Sherrell is registered through the National Yoga Alliance, Holy Yoga Ministries, and a Certified Group Fitness Instructor through the Aerobics & Fitness Association of America (AFAA). Her background consists of studies in Christian meditation, Pilates, Traditional and Holy Yoga, Thai Yoga Bodywork, and Modern Dance.

Sherrell is also an AFAA Certified Group Fitness Instructor, and a registered Holy Yoga Instructor. For more information please visit www.sherrellmooretucker.com.

www.ingramcontent.com/pod-product-compliance
Lightning Source LLC
LaVergne TN
LVHW021617080426
835510LV00019B/2616